I0426169

Evaluation of the Sensitivity of Inventory and Monitoring National Parks to Acidification Effects from Atmospheric Sulfur and Nitrogen Deposition

Eastern Rivers and Mountains Network (ERMN)

Natural Resource Report NPS/NRPC/ARD/NRR—2011/355

T. J. Sullivan
T. C. McDonnell
G. T. McPherson
S. D. Mackey
D. Moore

E&S Environmental Chemistry, Inc.
P.O. Box 609
Corvallis, OR 97339

April 2011

U.S. Department of the Interior
National Park Service
Natural Resource Program Center
Denver, Colorado

The National Park Service, Natural Resource Program Center publishes a range of reports that address natural resource topics of interest and applicability to a broad audience in the National Park Service and others in natural resource management, including scientists, conservation and environmental constituencies, and the public.

The Natural Resource Report Series is used to disseminate high-priority, current natural resource management information with managerial application. The series targets a general, diverse audience, and may contain NPS policy considerations or address sensitive issues of management applicability.

All manuscripts in the series receive the appropriate level of peer review to ensure that the information is scientifically credible, technically accurate, appropriately written for the intended audience, and designed and published in a professional manner.

This report received peer review by subject-matter experts who were not directly involved in the collection, analysis, or reporting of the data. Data in this report were collected and analyzed using methods based on established, peer-reviewed protocols and were analyzed and interpreted within the guidelines of the protocols.

Views, statements, findings, conclusions, recommendations, and data in this report do not necessarily reflect views and policies of the National Park Service, U.S. Department of the Interior. Mention of trade names or commercial products does not constitute endorsement or recommendation for use by the U.S. Government.

This report is available from Air Resources Division of the NPS (http://www.nature.nps.gov/air/Permits/ARIS/networks/acidification-eval.cfm) and the Natural Resource Publications Management website (http://www.nature.nps.gov/publications/nrpm/).

Please cite this publication as:

Sullivan, T. J., G. T. McPherson, T. C. McDonnell, S. D. Mackey, and D. Moore. 2011. Evaluation of the sensitivity of inventory and monitoring national parks to acidification effects from atmospheric sulfur and nitrogen deposition: Eastern Rivers and Mountains Network (ERMN). Natural Resource Report NPS/NRPC/ARD/NRR—2011/355. National Park Service, Denver, Colorado.

NPS 962/107390, April 2011

Eastern Rivers and Mountains Network (ERMN)

National maps of atmospheric S and N emissions and deposition are provided in Maps A through D as context for subsequent network data presentations. Maps A and B show county level emissions of total S and total N for the year 2002. Maps C and D show total S and total N deposition, again for the year 2002.

The Eastern Rivers and Mountains Network contains two parks that are slightly larger than 100 square miles: Delaware Water Gap (DEWA) and New River Gorge (NERI). In addition, there are seven smaller parks.

Total S and N emissions, by county, are shown in Maps E and F, respectively, for lands in and surrounding the Eastern Rivers and Mountains Network. County-level annual S emissions within the network were mostly less than 20 tons per square mile per year, although several counties showed higher emissions levels, up to more than 100 tons per square mile per year in some areas. Several counties just outside the network boundary also had S emission values exceeding 100 tons per square mile per year, predominately on the western border of the network (Map E). County-level annual N emissions within the network ranged from less than 1 ton per square mile to greater than 100 tons per square mile. In general, however, county annual N emissions were between 1 and 20 tons per square mile. A number of counties along the western border of the network showed total N annual emissions higher than 50 tons per square mile. Point source emissions of SO_2 and oxidized (nitrogen oxides, NO_x) and reduced (ammonia, NH_3) N, are shown in Maps G and H, respectively. There were many S point sources of substantial magnitude within the network, and a few just west of the network. Some emitted in excess of 40,000 tons of S per year (Map G). Most S point sources in the network ranged from less than 1 ton of S per year to 20,000 tons of S per year. The largest N point sources were consistently sources of oxidized, rather than reduced, N. Many NO_x point sources in and around the network were larger than 5,000 tons per year, mainly located in the mid-section of the network.

Urban centers within the network and within a 300-mile buffer around the network are shown on Map I. There are no population centers within the network that are larger than 500,000 people except Philadelphia, which is on the network border. There are several cities with populations between 100,000 and 500,000.

Spatial patterns in total S and N deposition are shown in maps J and K, respectively, for areas in and around the network. Included in this analysis are both wet and dry forms of deposition and both the oxidized and reduced N species. Total S deposition was quite high in comparison to other networks, with most of the network ranging from 15 to 20 kg S/ha/yr to greater than 30 kg S/ha/yr (Map J). Only a small portion of the network (in the southeast) had S deposition below 10 kg S/ha/yr. Total N deposition within the network ranged from as low as 5 to 10 kg N/ha/yr to as high as 15 to 20 kg N/ha/yr (Map K). Most of the network received 10 to 15 kg/ha/yr of total N deposition.

Land cover in and around the network is shown in Map L. The predominant cover types within this network are generally forest, pasture/hay, developed areas, and row crops.

In general, land slope tends to be moderately steep across park lands in this network, with average slope in the range of 10° to 30° (Map M). There are two parks, New River Gorge (NERI) and Bluestone (BLUE) that have slopes in the 30° to 40° range.

Park lands requiring special protection against potential adverse impacts associated with acidification from acidic deposition are shown on Map N. Also shown on Map N are all federal lands designated as wilderness, both lands managed by NPS and lands managed by other federal agencies. The land designations used to identify this heightened protection included Class I designation under the Clean Air Act Amendments and wilderness designation. There are no Class I areas in this network and only limited designated wilderness, none of which is on lands managed by NPS.

Network rankings are given in Figures A through C as the average ranking of the Pollutant Exposure, Ecosystem Sensitivity, and Park Protection metrics, respectively. Figure D shows the overall network Summary Risk ranking. In each figure, the rank for this particular network is highlighted to show its relative position compared with the ranks of the other 31 networks.

The Eastern Rivers and Mountains Network ranked Very High, in the middle of the top quintile, in Pollutant Exposure (Figure A). Sulfur and N emissions and deposition within the network were both high. The network Ecosystem Sensitivity ranking was also Very High, ranked at the bottom of the top quintile among networks (Figure B). This is because the geology and water within this network are known to be acid-sensitive, there are acid-sensitive tree species present, and slopes are steep, giving rise to low-order, relatively high-elevation streams. This network ranked in the lowest quintile in Park Protection, however, having limited amounts of protected lands (Figure C).

In combination, the network rankings for Pollutant Exposure, Ecosystem Sensitivity, and Park Protection yielded an overall Network Risk ranking that was relatively high compared with other networks (Figure D). The overall level of concern for acidification effects on I&M parks within this network is considered High.

Similarly, park rankings are given in Figures E through H for the same metrics. In the case of the park rankings, we only show in the figures the parks that are larger than 100 square miles. Relative ranks for all parks, including the smaller parks, are given in Table A and Appendix A. As for the network ranking figures, the park ranking figures highlight those parks that occur in this network to show their relative position compared with parks in the other 31 networks. Note that the rankings shown in Figures E through H reflect the rank of a given park compared with all other parks, irrespective of size.

The two I&M parks in the Eastern Rivers and Mountains Network that are larger than 100 square miles, DEWA and NERI, were ranked Very High among parks in Pollutant Exposure (Figure E). All but two of the smaller parks were ranked Very High for Pollutant Exposure; Bluestone (BLUE) and Upper Delaware (UPDE), were ranked as High. All of the parks in this network ranked Very High in Ecosystem Sensitivity, except Friendship Hill (FRHI), which was ranked Moderate for this theme. Park Protection rankings for all parks in the network were Moderate (Table A, Figure G). The Summary Risk ranking for six of the parks in this network (including DEWA and NERI) was Very High (Figure H, Table A). The other three parks were ranked High for Summary Risk.

Table A. Relative rankings of individual I&M parks within the network for Pollutant Exposure, Ecosystem Sensitivity, Park Protection, and overall Summary Risk from acidic deposition.

I&M Parks[2] in Network	Relative Ranking of Individual Parks[1]			
	Pollutant Exposure	Ecosystem Sensitivity	Park Protection	Summary Risk
Allegheny Portage Railroad	Very High	Very High	Moderate	Very High
Bluestone	High	Very High	Moderate	High
Delaware Water Gap	Very High	Very High	Moderate	Very High
Fort Necessity	Very High	Very High	Moderate	Very High
Friendship Hill	Very High	Moderate	Moderate	High
Gauley River	Very High	Very High	Moderate	Very High
Johnstown Flood	Very High	Very High	Moderate	Very High
New River Gorge	Very High	Very High	Moderate	Very High
Upper Delaware	High	Very High	Moderate	High

[1] Relative park rankings are designated according to quintile ranking, among all I&M Parks, from the lowest quintile (very low risk) to the highest quintile (very high risk).

[2] Park name is printed in bold italic for parks larger than 100 square miles.

Map A.   National map of total S emissions by county for the year 2002, in units of tons of S per square mile per year. (Source of data: EPA National Emissions Inventory, http://www.epa.gov/ttn/chief/net/2002inventory.html)

Map B.   National map of total N emissions by county for the year 2002. Both oxidized (nitrogen oxides, NO_x) and reduced (ammonia, NH_3) forms of N are included. The total is expressed in tons per square mile per year. (Source of data: EPA National Emissions Inventory, http://www.epa.gov/ttn/chief/net/2002inventory.html)

Map C.   Total S deposition for the conterminous United States for the year 2002, expressed in units of kilograms of S deposited from the atmosphere to the Earth surface per hectare per year. For the eastern half of the country, wet deposition values were derived from interpolated measured values from NADP (three-year average centered on 2002) and dry deposition values were derived from 12-km CMAQ model projections for 2002. For the western half of the country, both wet and dry deposition values were derived from 36-km CMAQ model projections for 2002. NADP interpolations were performed using the approach of Grimm and Lynch (1997). CMAQ model projections were provided by Robin Dennis, U.S. EPA.

Map D.   Total N deposition for the conterminous United States for the year 2002, expressed in units of kilograms of N deposited from the atmosphere to the Earth surface per hectare per year. Wet and dry forms of both oxidized (nitrogen oxides, NO_x) and reduced (ammonia, NH_3) N are included. For the eastern half of the country, wet deposition values were derived from interpolated measured values from NADP (three-year average centered on 2002) and dry deposition values were derived from 12-km CMAQ model projections for 2002. For the western half of the country, both wet and dry deposition values were derived from 36-km CMAQ model projections for 2002. NADP interpolations were performed using the approach of Grimm and Lynch (1997). CMAQ model projections were provided by Robin Dennis, U.S. EPA.

Map E. Total S emissions by county for lands surrounding the network, expressed as tons of S emitted into the atmosphere per square mile per year. (Source of data: EPA National Emissions Inventory, http://www.epa.gov/ttn/chief/net/2002inventory.html)

Map F. Total N emissions by county for lands surrounding the network, expressed as tons of N emitted into the atmosphere per square mile per year. The total includes both oxidized (nitrogen oxides, NO_x) and reduced (ammonia, NH_3) N. (Source of data: EPA National Emissions Inventory, http://www.epa.gov/ttn/chief/net/2002inventory.html)

Map G. Major point source emissions of SO_2 for lands surrounding the network. (Source of data: EPA National Emissions Inventory, http://www.epa.gov/ttn/chief/net/2002inventory.html)

Map H. Major point source emissions of oxidized (nitrogen oxides, NO_x) and reduced (ammonia, NH_3) N in and around the network. The base of each vertical bar is positioned in the map at the approximate location of the source. The height of the bar is proportional to the magnitude of the source. (Source of data: EPA National Emissions Inventory, http://www.epa.gov/ttn/chief/net/2002inventory.html)

Map I. Urban centers having more than 10,000 people within the network and within a 300-mile buffer around the perimeter of the network. (Source of data: U.S. Census 2000)

Map J. Total S deposition in and around the network. Values are expressed as kilograms of S deposited per hectare per year. (Source of data: Interpolated NADP wet and CMAQ Model dry deposition data for 2002; see information for Map C above for details)

Map K. Total N deposition in and around the network. Included in the total are wet plus dry forms of both oxidized (nitrogen oxides, NO_x) and reduced (ammonia, NH_3) N. Values are expressed as kilograms of N deposited per hectare per year. (Source of data: Interpolated NADP wet and CMAQ Model dry deposition data for 2002; see information for Map D above for details)

Map L. Land cover types in and around the network, based on the National Land Cover dataset. (Source of data: National Land Cover Dataset, http://www.mrlc.gov/nlcd_multizone_map.php)

Map M. Average land slope within park units that occur within the network, by 10-digit HUC. (Source of data: U.S. EPA National Elevation Dataset [http://ned.usgs.gov/])

Map N.   Lands within the network that are classified as Class I or wilderness area. (Source of data: USGS 2005 [National Atlas; http://nationalatlas.gov] and NPS)

Figure A.   Network rankings for Pollutant Exposure, calculated as the average of scores for all Pollutant Exposure variables.

Figure B.   Network rankings for Ecosystem Sensitivity, calculated as the average of scores for all Ecosystem Sensitivity variables.

Figure C.   Network rankings for Park Protection, calculated as the average of scores for all Park Protection variables.

Figure D.   Network Summary Risk rankings, calculated as the average of the quintile ranks for the Pollutant Exposure, Ecosystem Sensitivity, and Park Protection themes.

Figure E.   Park rankings for Pollutant Exposure for all parks larger than 100 square miles. Ranks for each park were calculated relative to all parks, regardless of size, as the average of scores for all Pollutant Exposure variables.

Figure F.   Park rankings for Ecosystem Sensitivity for all parks larger than 100 square miles. Ranks for each park were calculated relative to all parks, regardless of size, as the average of scores for all Ecosystem Sensitivity variables.

Figure G.   Park rankings for Park Protection for all parks larger than 100 square miles. Ranks for each park were calculated relative to all parks, regardless of size, as the average of scores for all Park Protection variables.

Figure H.   Park rankings for Summary Risk for all parks larger than 100 square miles. Ranks for each park were calculated relative to all parks, regardless of size, as the average of the quintile ranks for the Pollutant Exposure, Ecosystem Sensitivity, and Park Protection themes.

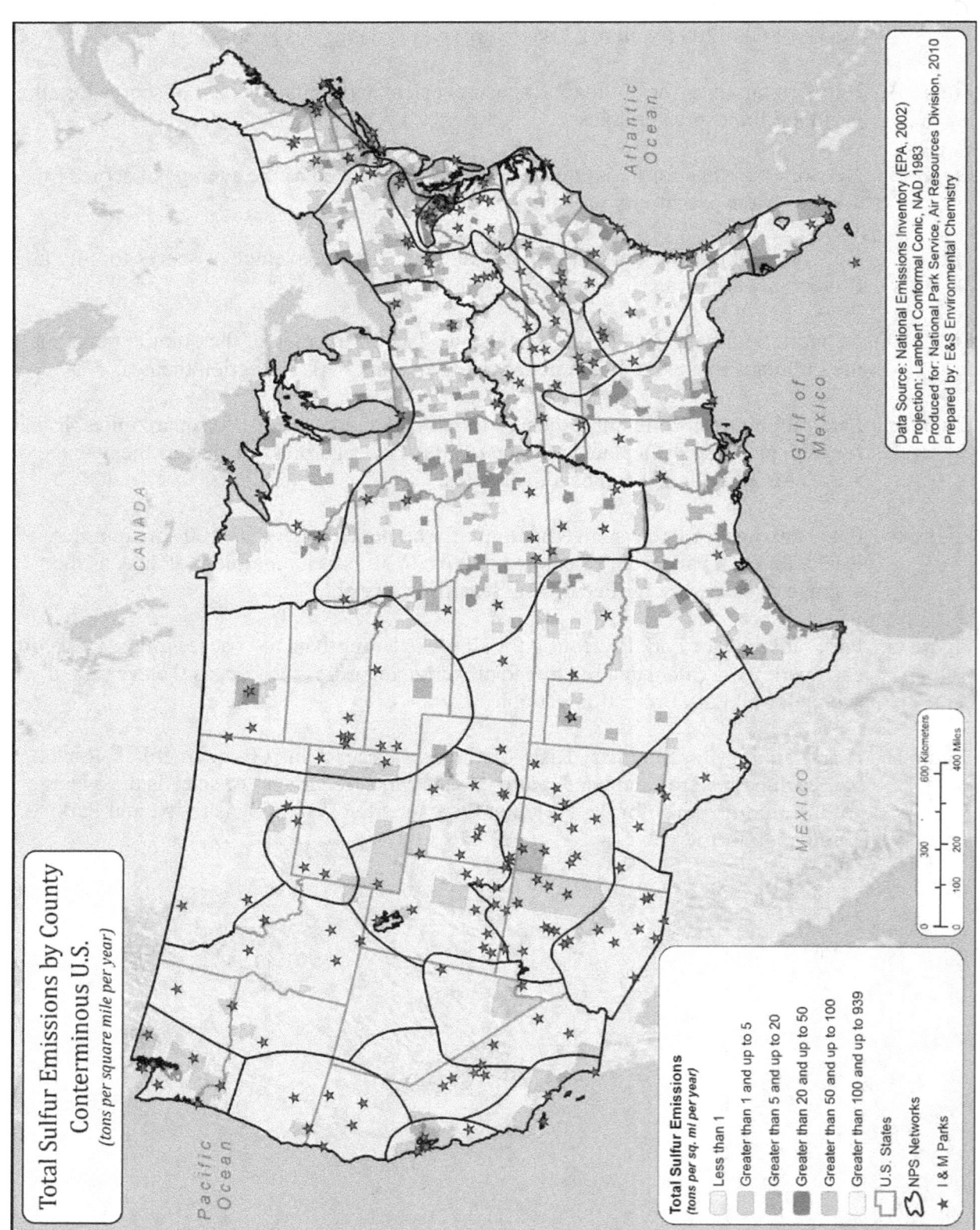

Total Sulfur Emissions by County
Conterminous U.S.
(tons per square mile per year)

Total Sulfur Emissions
(tons per sq. mi per year)

Less than 1
Greater than 1 and up to 5
Greater than 5 and up to 20
Greater than 20 and up to 50
Greater than 50 and up to 100
Greater than 100 and up to 939
U.S. States
NPS Networks
★ I & M Parks

Data Source: National Emissions Inventory (EPA, 2002)
Projection: Lambert Conformal Conic, NAD 1983
Produced for: National Park Service, Air Resources Division, 2010
Prepared by: E&S Environmental Chemistry

CANADA

MEXICO

Pacific Ocean

Atlantic Ocean

Gulf of Mexico

600 Kilometers
400 Miles
0   100   200   300
0

Map A

Total Nitrogen Emissions by County
Conterminous U.S.
(tons per sq. mi per year)

Total Nitrogen Emissions
(tons per sq. mi per year)

Less than 1
Greater than 1 and up to 5
Greater than 5 and up to 20
Greater than 20 and up to 50
Greater than 50 and up to 100
Greater than 100 and up to 618
U.S. States
NPS Networks
★ I & M Parks

Data Source: National Emissions Inventory (EPA, 2002)
Projection: Lambert Conformal Conic, NAD 1983
Produced for: National Park Service, Air Resources Division, 2010
Prepared by: E&S Environmental Chemistry

Map B

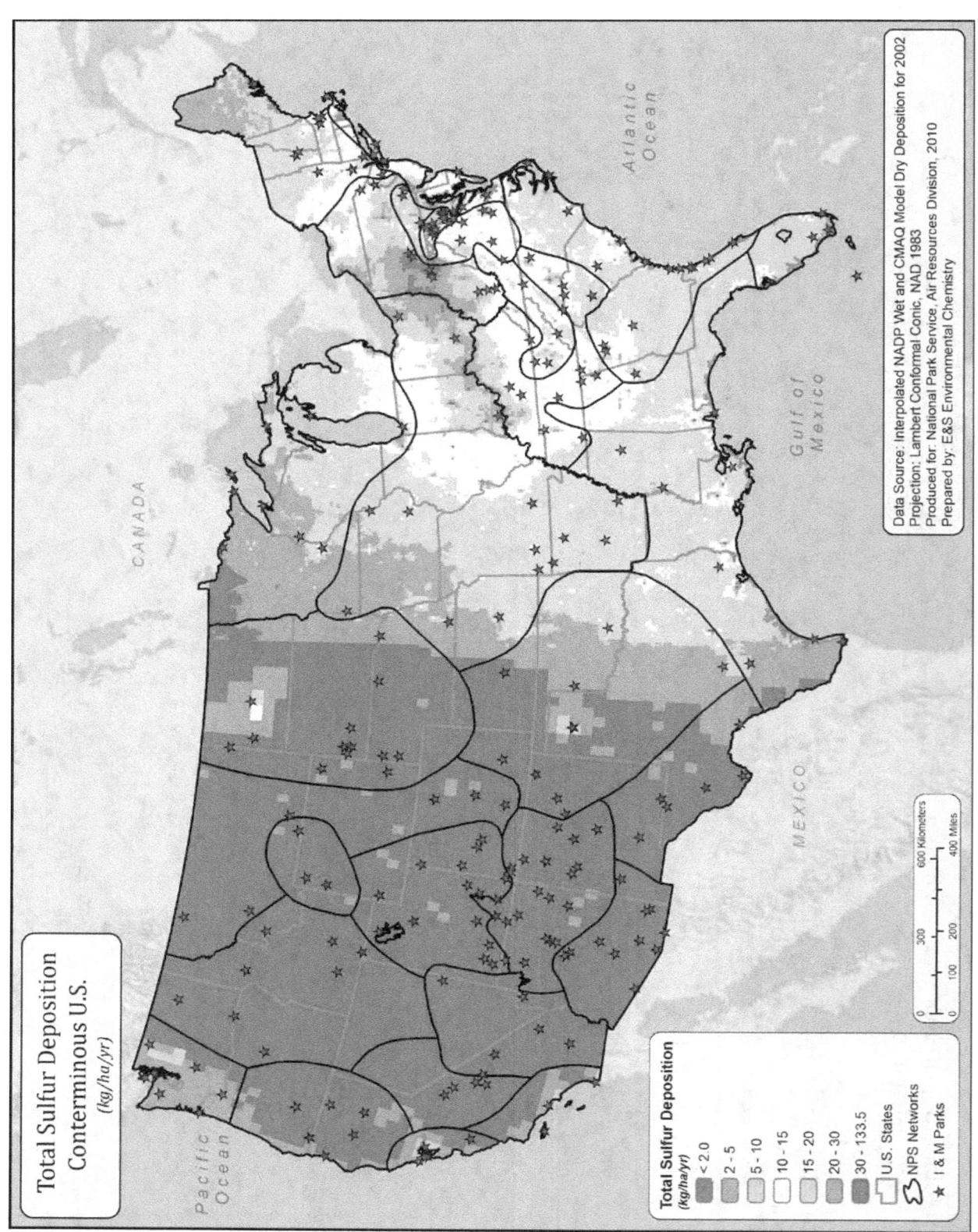

Total Sulfur Deposition
Conterminous U.S.
(kg/ha/yr)

Total Sulfur Deposition
(kg/ha/yr)
- < 2.0
- 2 - 5
- 5 - 10
- 10 - 15
- 15 - 20
- 20 - 30
- 30 - 133.5
- U.S. States
- NPS Networks
- ★ I & M Parks

Data Source: Interpolated NADP Wet and CMAQ Model Dry Deposition for 2002
Projection: Lambert Conformal Conic, NAD 1983
Produced for: National Park Service, Air Resources Division, 2010
Prepared by: E&S Environmental Chemistry

Map C

Total Nitrogen Deposition
Conterminous U.S.
(kg/ha/yr)

Total Nitrogen Deposition
(kg/ha/yr)
- < 2.0
- 2 - 5
- 5 - 10
- 10 - 15
- 15 - 20
- 20 - 30
- 30 - 63.5
- U.S. States
- NPS Networks
- I & M Parks

Data Source: Interpolated NADP Wet and CMAQ Model Dry Deposition for 2002
Projection: Lambert Conformal Conic, NAD 1983
Produced for: National Park Service, Air Resources Division, 2010
Prepared by: E&S Environmental Chemistry

Map D

Total Sulfur Emissions by County

Eastern Rivers and Mountains Network

(tons per square mile per year)

Locator Map

Total S Emissions *(tons per sq. mi per year)*

- Less than 1
- Greater than 1 and up to 5
- Greater than 5 and up to 20
- Greater than 20 and up to 50
- Greater than 50 and up to 100
- Greater than 100 and up to 939
- U.S. States
- Eastern Rivers and Mountains Network
- Network Parks (larger than 100 sq. mi)
- Network Parks (smaller than 100 sq. mi)

0   25   50 Kilometers
0   25   50 Miles

Data Source: National Emissions Inventory (EPA, 2002)
Projection: Lambert Conformal Conic, NAD 1983
Produced for: National Park Service, Air Resources Division, 2010
Prepared by: E&S Environmental Chemistry

NY
NJ
MD
PA
VA
VA
WV
KY
OH
MI
IN
CANADA
Lake Ontario
Lake Erie

Map E

Total Nitrogen Emissions by County Eastern Rivers and Mountains Network

(tons per square mile per year)

Locator Map

Total N Emissions *(tons per sq. mi per year)*

- Less than 1
- Greater than 1 and up to 5
- Greater than 5 and up to 20
- Greater than 20 and up to 50
- Greater than 50 and up to 100
- Greater than 100 and up to 618
- U.S. States
- Eastern Rivers and Mountains Network
- ☆ Network Parks (larger than 100 sq. mi)
- ★ Network Parks (smaller than 100 sq. mi)

Lake Ontario

Lake Erie

CANADA

N Y

N J

P A

M D

W V

K Y

M I

O H

I N

0   25   50 Kilometers
0   25   50 Miles

Data Source: National Emissions Inventory (EPA, 2002)
Projection: Lambert Conformal Conic, NAD 1983
Produced for: National Park Service, Air Resources Division, 2010
Prepared by: E&S Environmental Chemistry

Map F

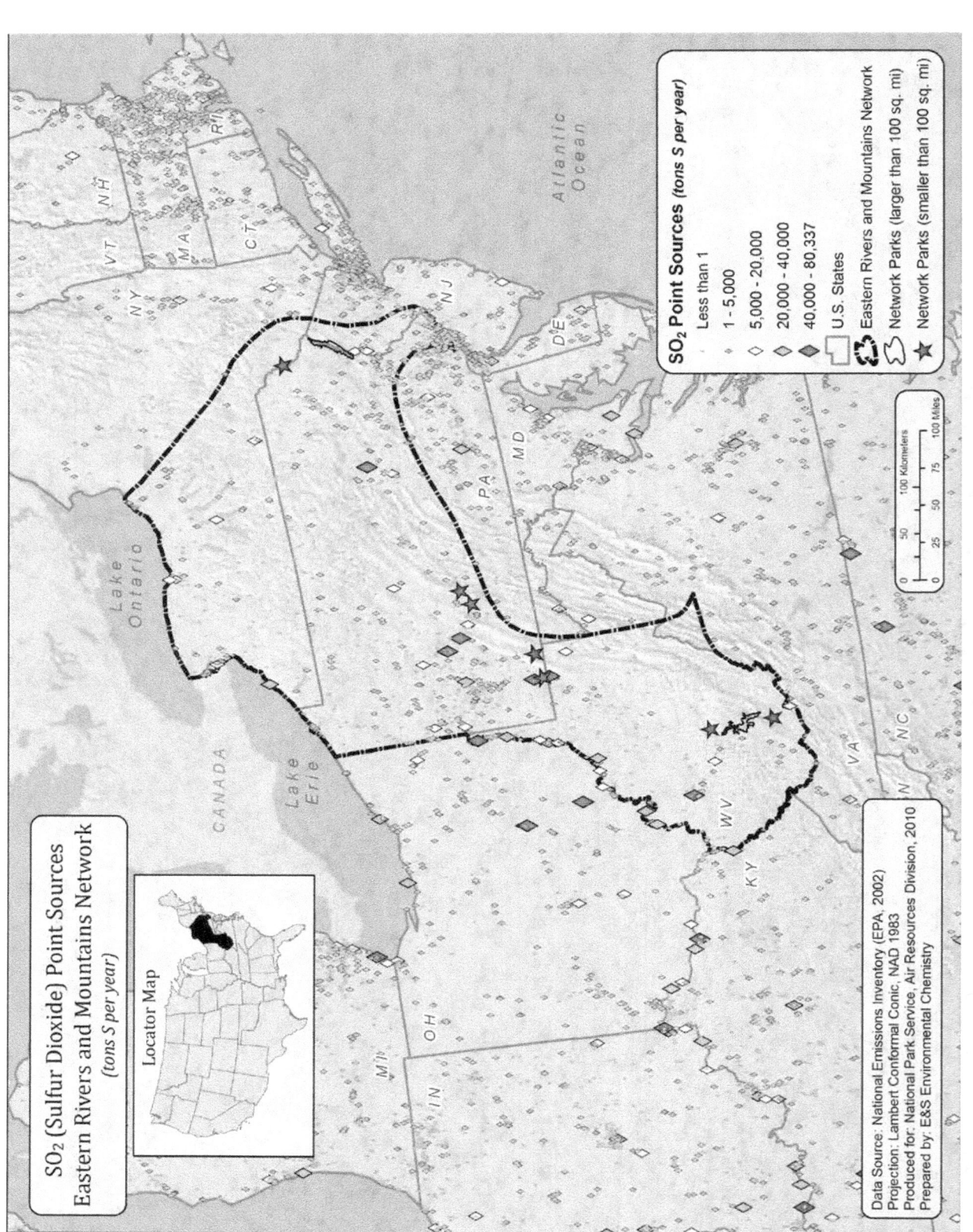

SO₂ (Sulfur Dioxide) Point Sources
Eastern Rivers and Mountains Network
(tons S per year)

Locator Map

SO₂ Point Sources *(tons S per year)*

Less than 1
1 - 5,000
5,000 - 20,000
20,000 - 40,000
40,000 - 80,337

U.S. States
Eastern Rivers and Mountains Network
Network Parks (larger than 100 sq. mi)
Network Parks (smaller than 100 sq. mi)

Atlantic Ocean

CANADA

Lake Ontario

Lake Erie

NY
VT
NH
MA
RI
CT
NJ
DE
MD
PA
WV
VA
NC
KY
OH
IN
MI

0 25 50 75 100 Miles
0 50 100 Kilometers

Data Source: National Emissions Inventory (EPA, 2002)
Projection: Lambert Conformal Conic, NAD 1983
Produced for: National Park Service, Air Resources Division, 2010
Prepared by: E&S Environmental Chemistry

Map G

ERMN-12

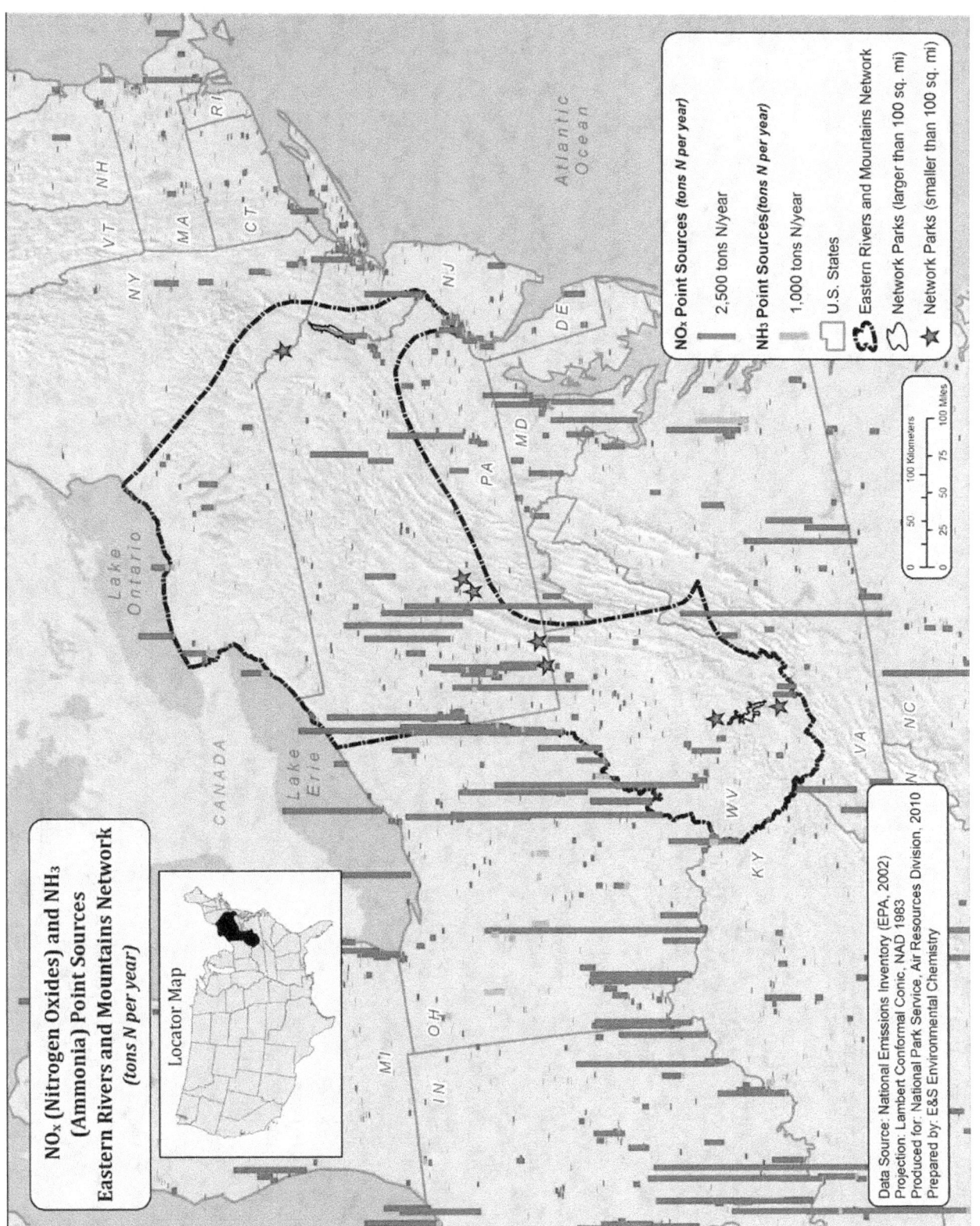

NO$_x$ (Nitrogen Oxides) and NH$_3$ (Ammonia) Point Sources
Eastern Rivers and Mountains Network
(tons N per year)

Locator Map

NO$_x$ Point Sources *(tons N per year)*

— 2,500 tons N/year

NH$_3$ Point Sources *(tons N per year)*

— 1,000 tons N/year

☐ U.S. States

Eastern Rivers and Mountains Network

Network Parks (larger than 100 sq. mi)

Network Parks (smaller than 100 sq. mi)

Data Source: National Emissions Inventory (EPA, 2002)
Projection: Lambert Conformal Conic, NAD 1983
Produced for: National Park Service, Air Resources Division, 2010
Prepared by: E&S Environmental Chemistry

Atlantic Ocean

CANADA

Lake Ontario

Lake Erie

NY, VT, NH, MA, CT, RI, NJ, DE, MD, PA, WV, VA, KY, OH, IN, MI, N C

0 25 50 75 100 Miles
0 50 100 Kilometers

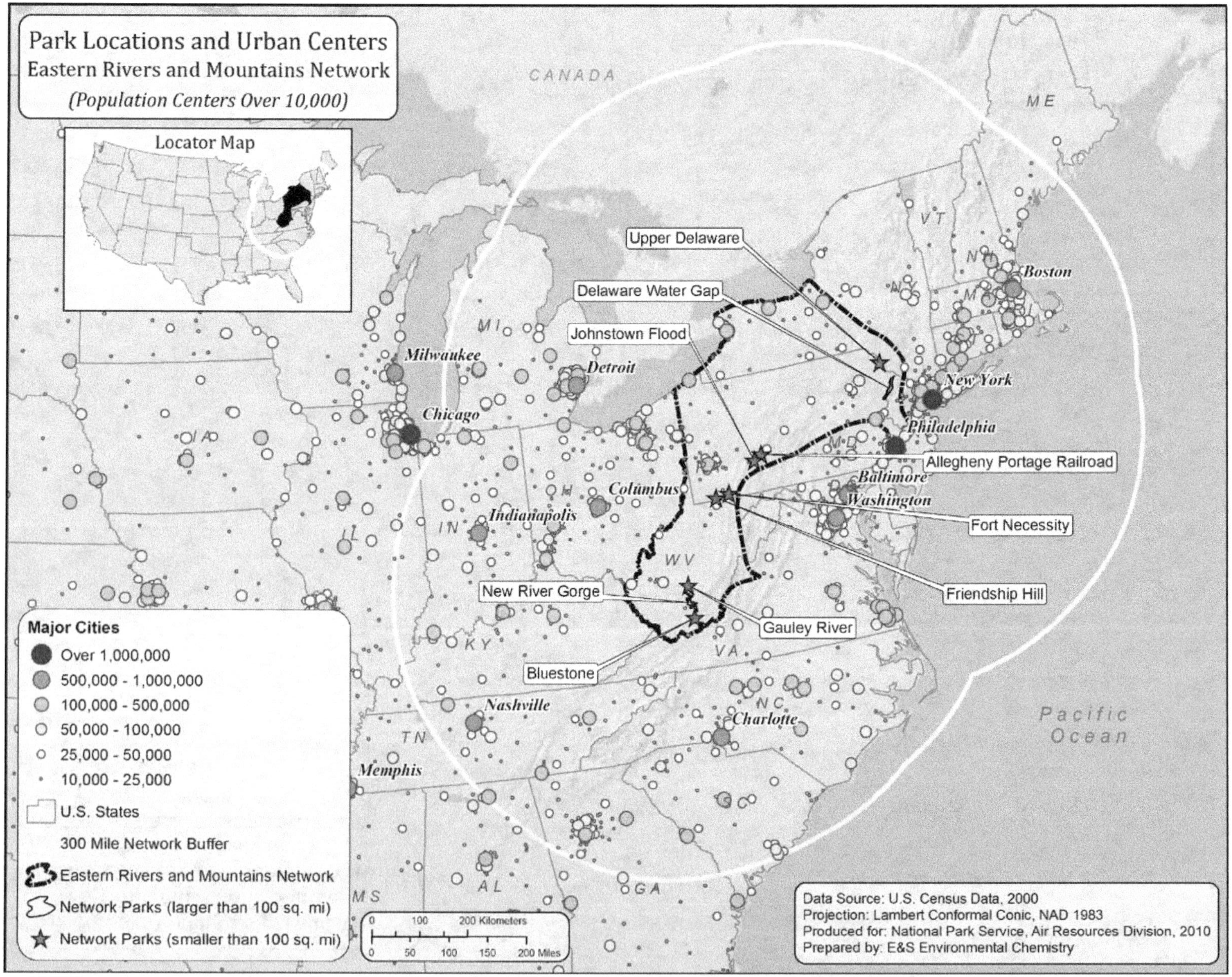

Park Locations and Urban Centers
Eastern Rivers and Mountains Network
(Population Centers Over 10,000)

Map I

ERMN-14

Total Sulfur Deposition
Eastern Rivers and Mountains Network
(kg/ha/yr)

Locator Map

Total Sulfur Deposition

kg/ha/yr

- < 2.0
- 2 - 5
- 5 - 10
- 10 - 15
- 15 - 20
- 20 - 30
- 30 - 133.5
- U.S. States
- Eastern Rivers and Mountains Network
- Network Parks (larger than 100 sq. mi)
- ★ Network Parks (smaller than 100 sq. mi)

0   50   100 Kilometers

0   50   100 Miles

N Y

N J

Atlantic Ocean

M D

P A

Lake Ontario

CANADA

Lake Erie

K Y

W V

O H

I N

M I

Data Source: Interpolated NADP Wet and CMAQ Model Dry Deposition for 2002
Projection: Lambert Conformal Conic, NAD 1983
Produced for: National Park Service, Air Resources Division, 2010
Prepared by: E&S Environmental Chemistry

Map J

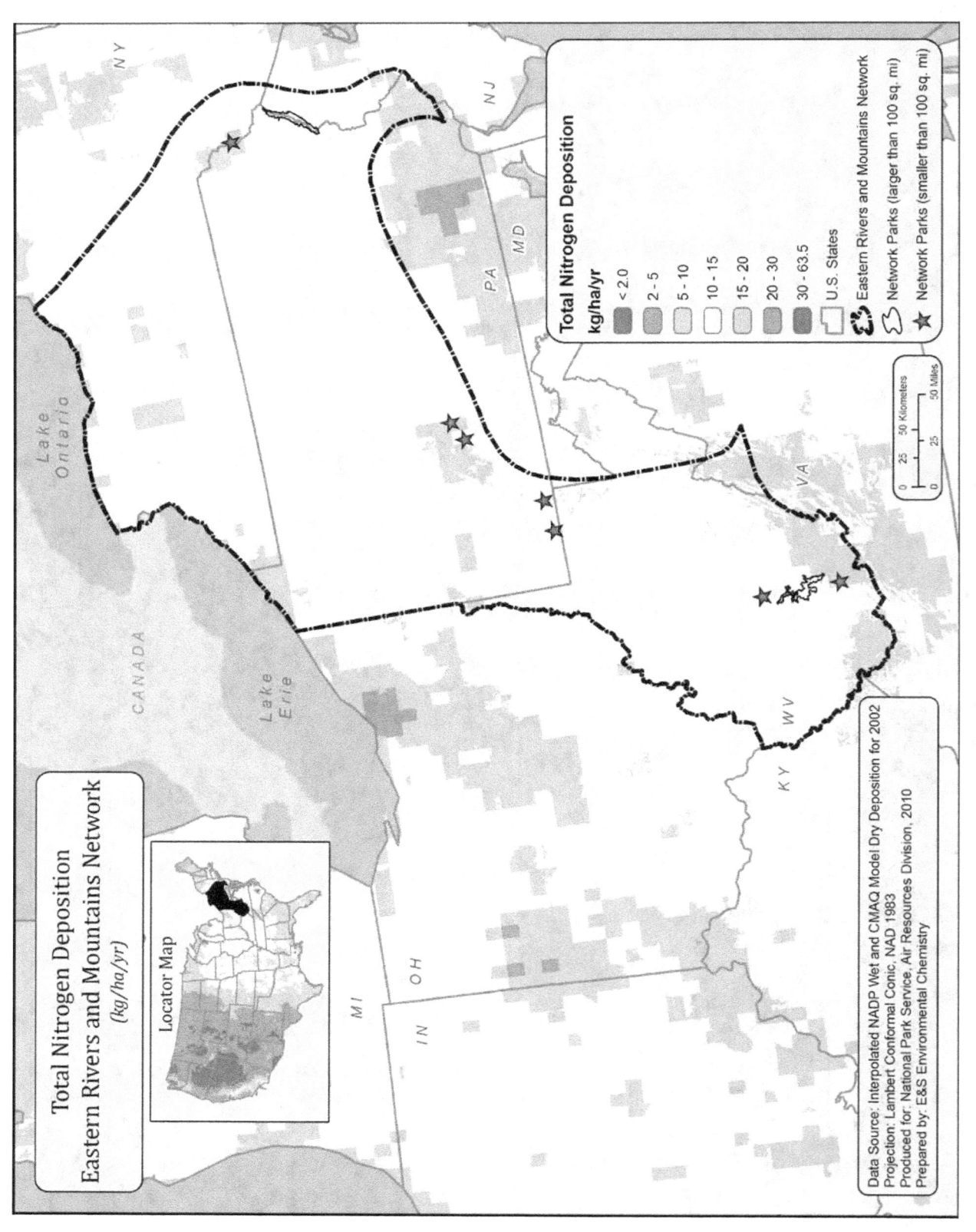

Total Nitrogen Deposition
Eastern Rivers and Mountains Network
(kg/ha/yr)

Locator Map

Total Nitrogen Deposition

kg/ha/yr
- < 2.0
- 2 - 5
- 5 - 10
- 10 - 15
- 15 - 20
- 20 - 30
- 30 - 63.5
- U.S. States

Eastern Rivers and Mountains Network

★ Network Parks (larger than 100 sq. mi)

★ Network Parks (smaller than 100 sq. mi)

0   25   50 Kilometers
0   25   50 Miles

Data Source: Interpolated NADP Wet and CMAQ Model Dry Deposition for 2002
Projection: Lambert Conformal Conic, NAD 1983
Produced for: National Park Service, Air Resources Division, 2010
Prepared by: E&S Environmental Chemistry

Map K

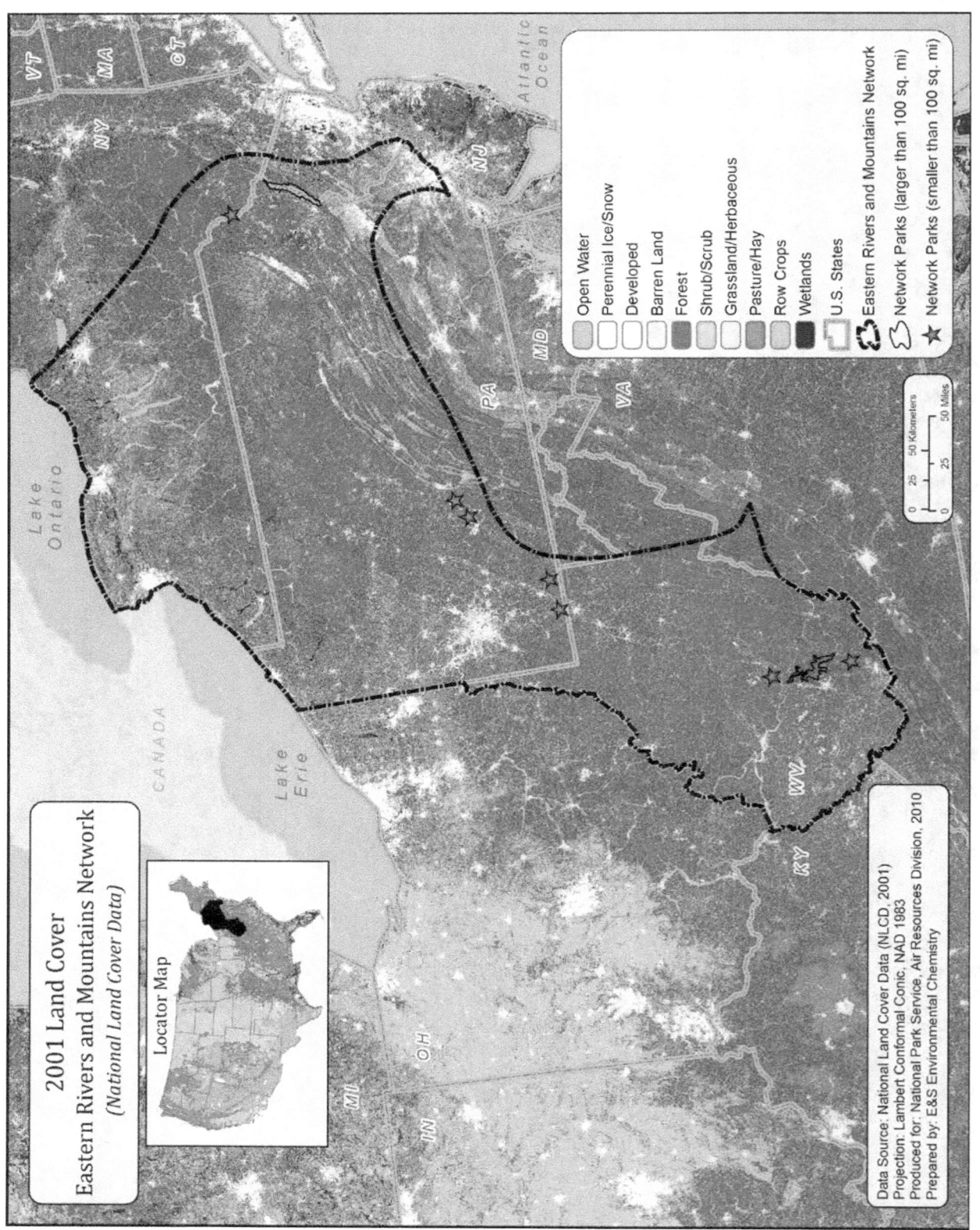

2001 Land Cover
Eastern Rivers and Mountains Network
(National Land Cover Data)

Locator Map

Open Water
Perennial Ice/Snow
Developed
Barren Land
Forest
Shrub/Scrub
Grassland/Herbaceous
Pasture/Hay
Row Crops
Wetlands
U.S. States

Eastern Rivers and Mountains Network
Network Parks (larger than 100 sq. mi)
Network Parks (smaller than 100 sq. mi)

Data Source: National Land Cover Data (NLCD, 2001)
Projection: Lambert Conformal Conic, NAD 1983
Produced for: National Park Service, Air Resources Division, 2010
Prepared by: E&S Environmental Chemistry

0   25   50 Kilometers
0   25   50 Miles

Atlantic Ocean
CANADA
Lake Ontario
Lake Erie

VT
MA
CT
NY
NJ
MD
PA
VA
WV
KY
OH
MI
IN

ERMN-18

Watershed Slope by Network
Eastern Rivers and Mountains Network
Coded by 10-Digit HUC Boundary

Locator Map

Watershed Slope (degrees)

Less than 10
10 - 20
20 - 30
30 - 40
40 - 50
Greater than 50
U.S. States
Eastern Rivers and Mountains Network
Network Parks (larger than 100 sq. mi)
I & M Parks (smaller than 100 sq. mi)

100 Kilometers
100 Miles

NY
NJ
PA
MD
VA
CANADA
Lake Ontario
Lake Erie
WV
KY
OH
IN
MI

Data Source: National Elevation Dataset (2006)
Projection: Lambert Conformal Conic, NAD 1983
Produced for: National Park Service, Air Resources Division, 2010
Prepared by: E&S Environmental Chemistry

Map M

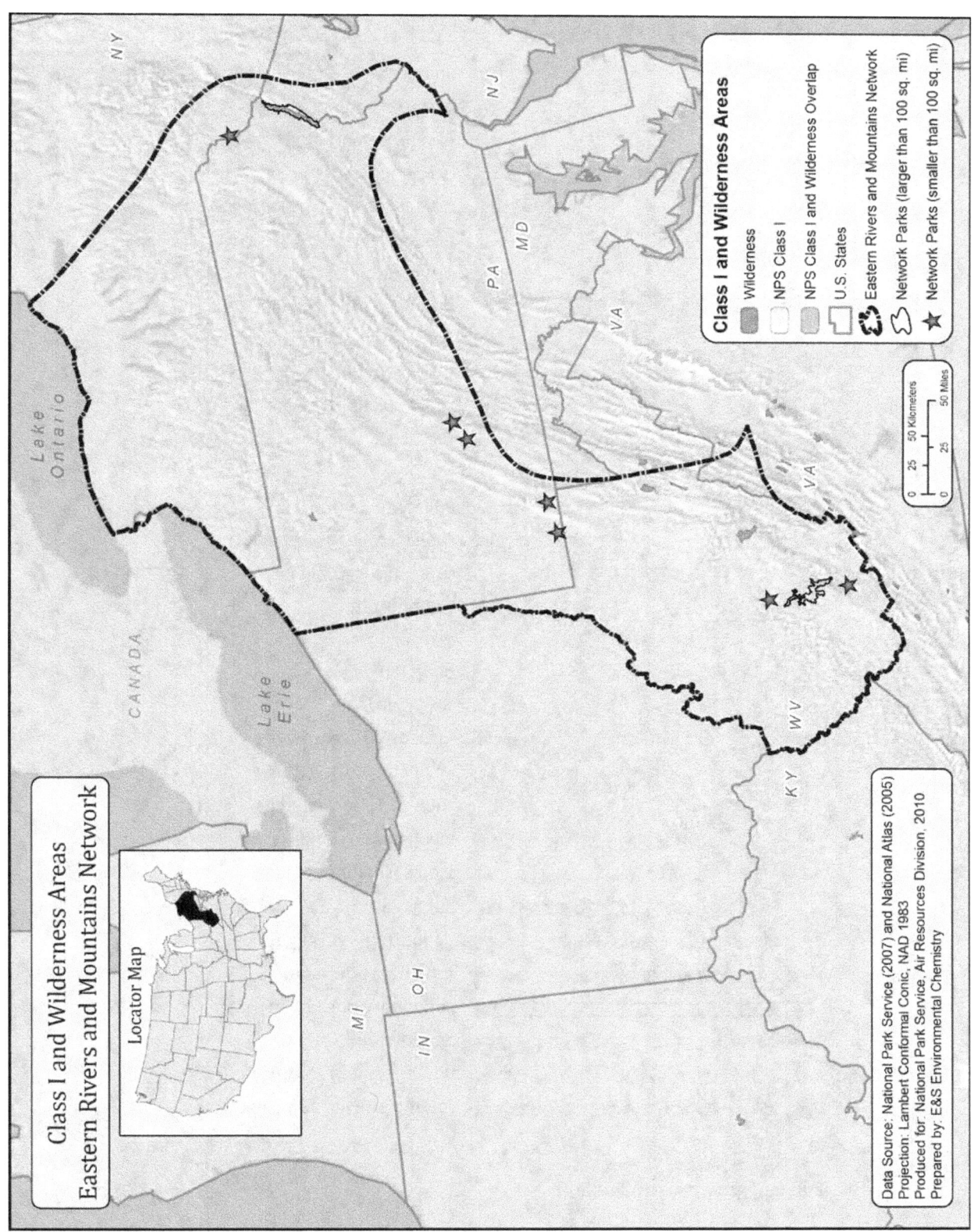

Class I and Wilderness Areas
Eastern Rivers and Mountains Network

Locator Map

Class I and Wilderness Areas

Wilderness
NPS Class I
NPS Class I and Wilderness Overlap
U.S. States
Eastern Rivers and Mountains Network
Network Parks (larger than 100 sq. mi)
Network Parks (smaller than 100 sq. mi)

Data Source: National Park Service (2007) and National Atlas (2005)
Projection: Lambert Conformal Conic, NAD 1983
Produced for: National Park Service, Air Resources Division, 2010
Prepared by: E&S Environmental Chemistry

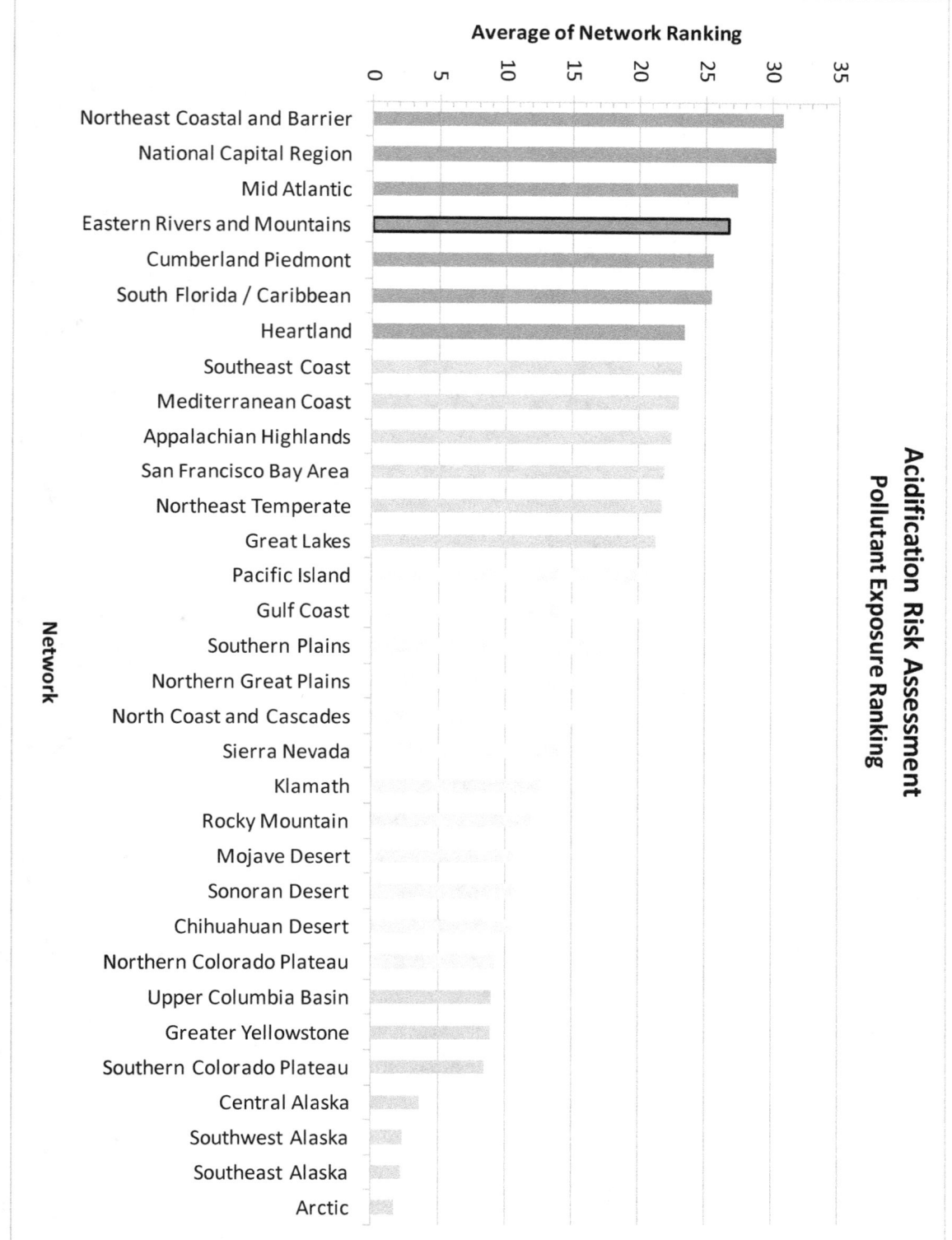

Figure A

Acidification Risk Assessment
Pollutant Exposure Ranking

Figure B

Acidification Risk Assessment
Ecosystem Sensitivity Ranking

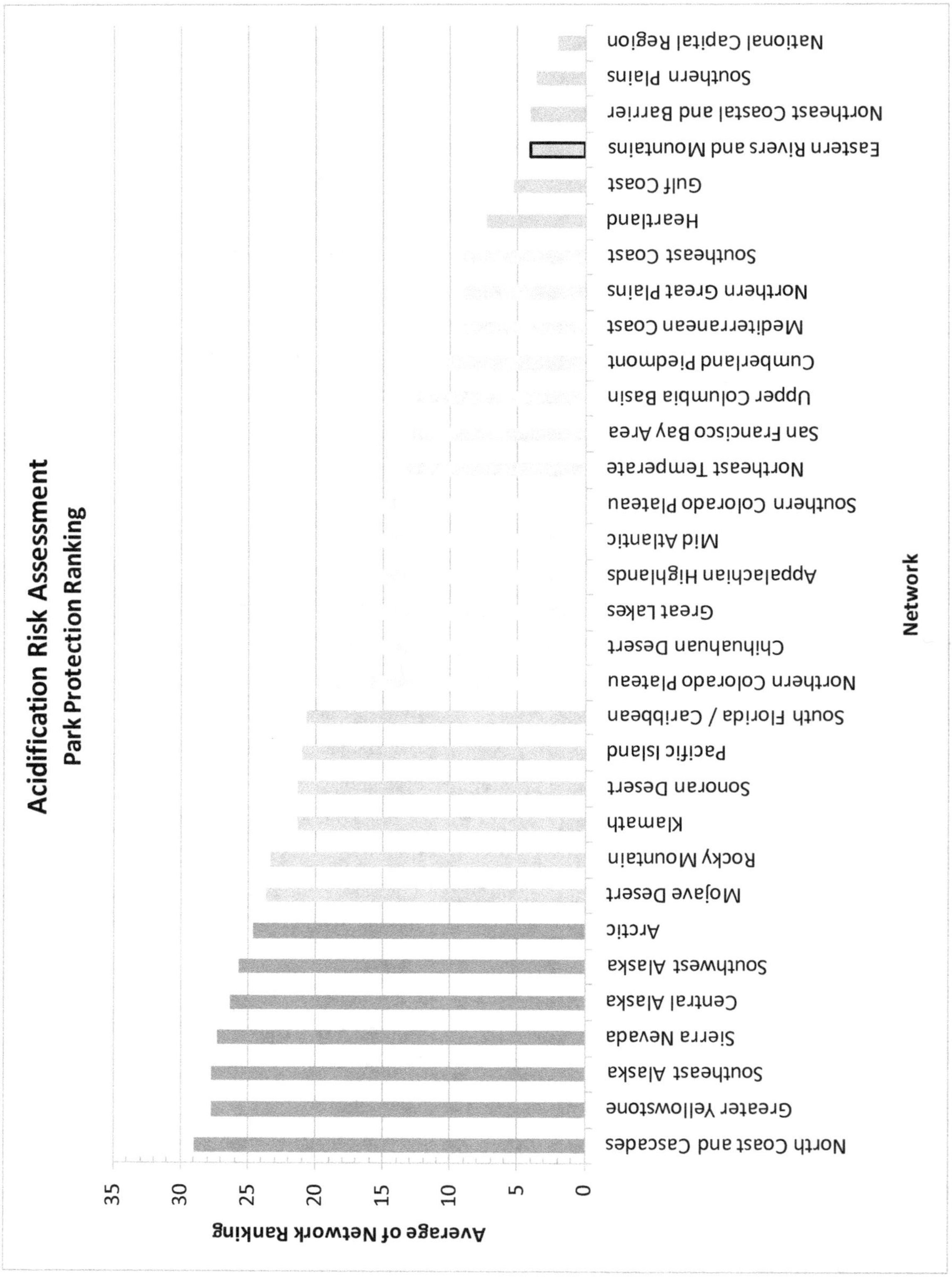
Acidification Risk Assessment
Park Protection Ranking
Average of Network Ranking
0
5
10
15
20
25
30
35
North Coast and Cascades
Greater Yellowstone
Southeast Alaska
Sierra Nevada
Central Alaska
Southwest Alaska
Arctic
Mojave Desert
Rocky Mountain
Klamath
Sonoran Desert
Pacific Island
South Florida / Caribbean
Northern Colorado Plateau
Chihuahuan Desert
Great Lakes
Appalachian Highlands
Mid Atlantic
Southern Colorado Plateau
Northeast Temperate
San Francisco Bay Area
Upper Columbia Basin
Cumberland Piedmont
Mediterranean Coast
Northern Great Plains
Southeast Coast
Heartland
Gulf Coast
Eastern Rivers and Mountains
Northeast Coastal and Barrier
Southern Plains
National Capital Region
Network

Figure C

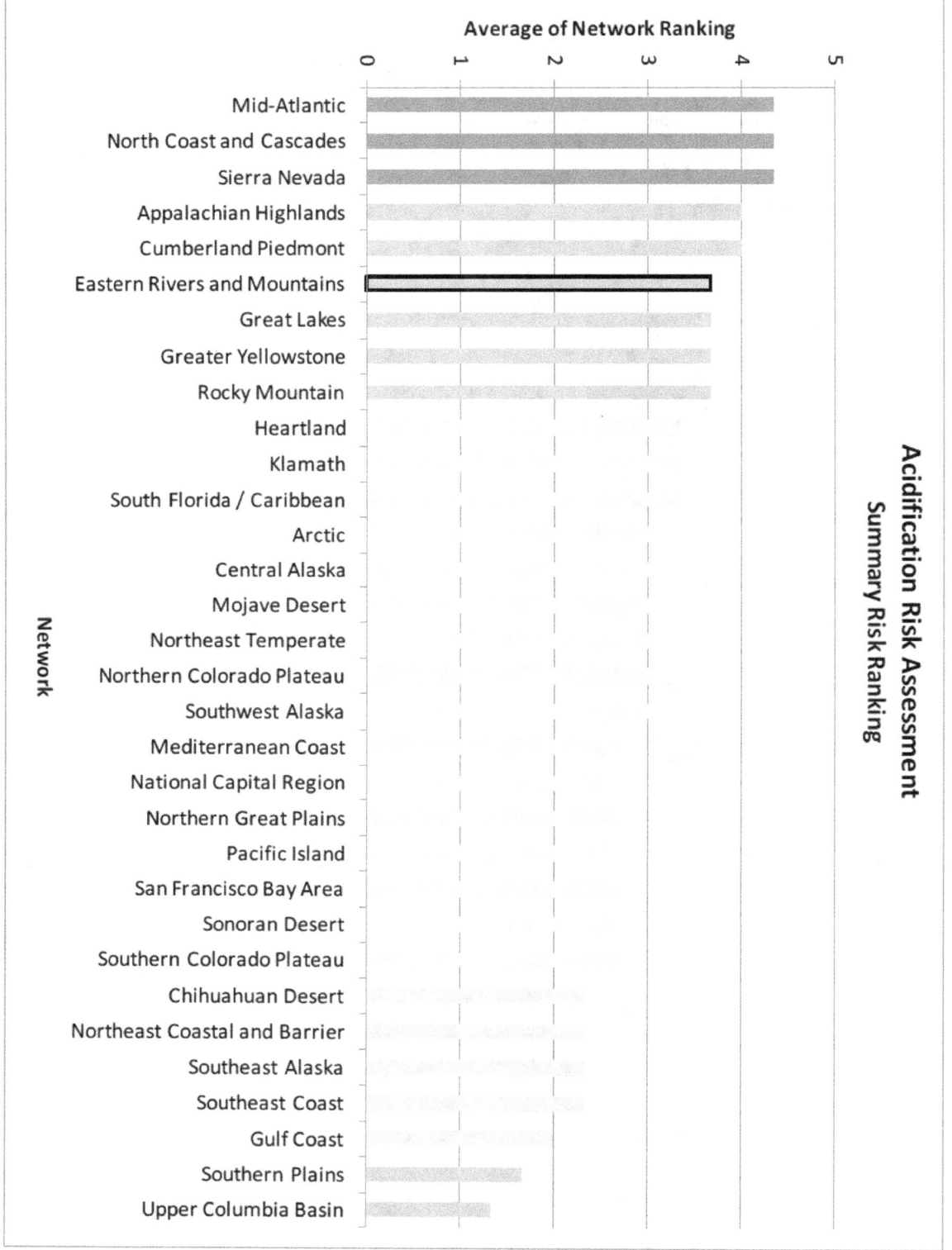

Figure D

Acidification Risk Assessment
Summary Risk Ranking

Figure E

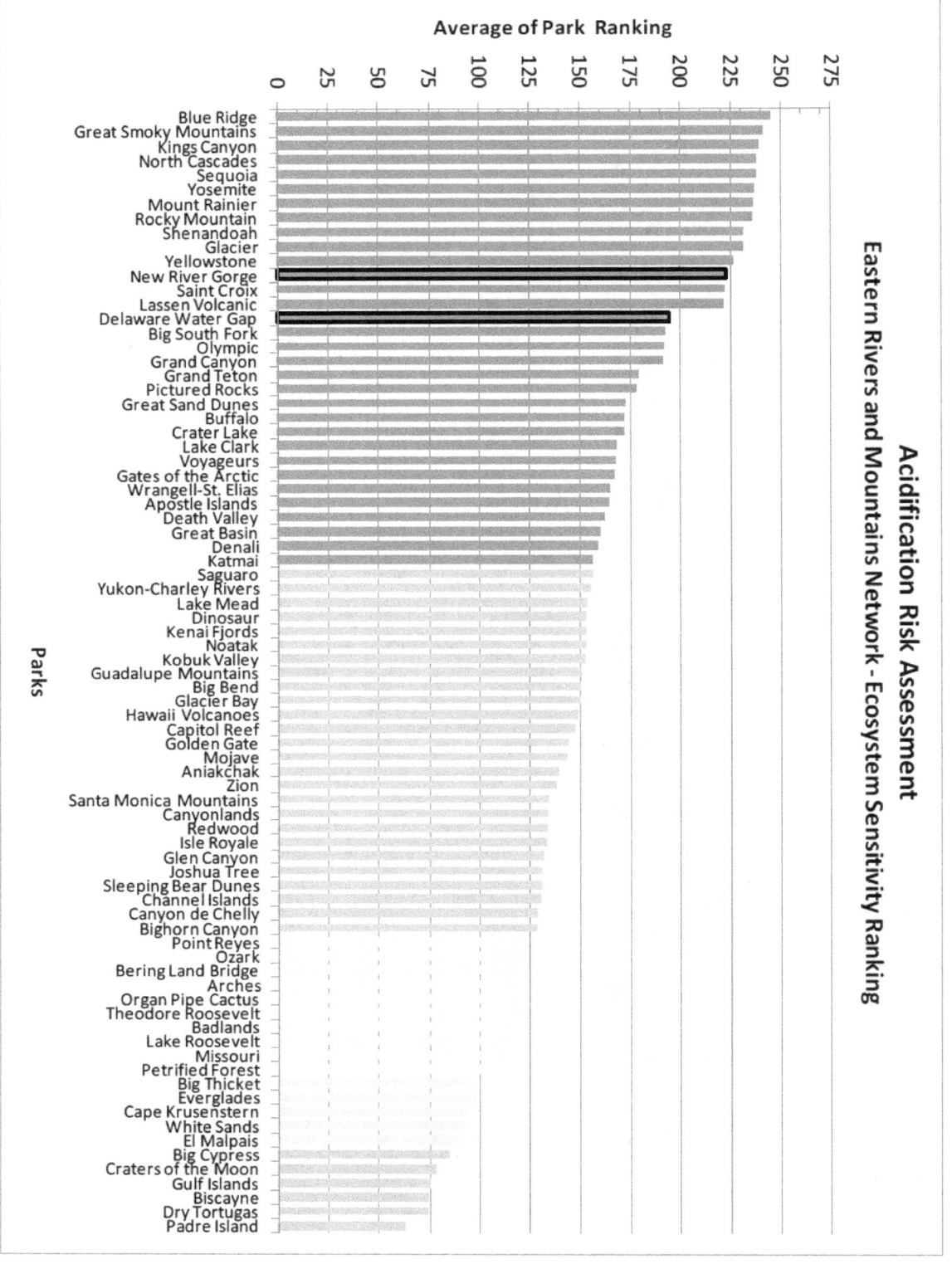

Figure F

Acidification Risk Assessment
Eastern Rivers and Mountains Network - Ecosystem Sensitivity Ranking

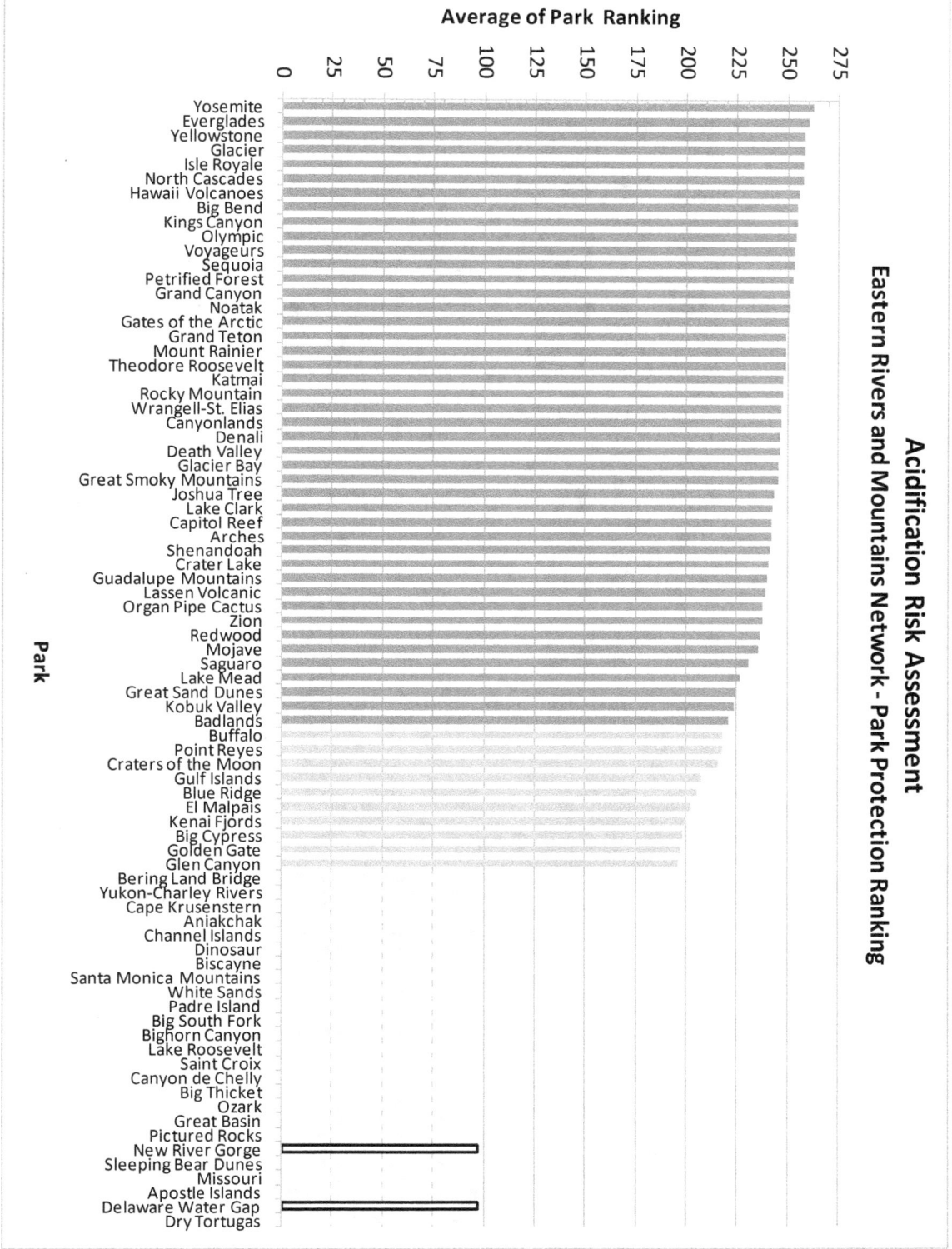

Figure G

Acidification Risk Assessment
Eastern Rivers and Mountains Network - Park Protection Ranking

Acidification Risk Assessment

Eastern Rivers and Mountains Network - Summary Risk Ranking

Figure H

NPS 962/107390, April 2011